Politics and Betrayal

Layered Voice Analysis for Newly Elected Leaders

Dale L. Tunnell, Ph.D.

Politics and Betrayal: Layered Voice Analysis for Newly Elected Leaders

Western Legends Research
P. O. Box 6 Wright, Wyoming 82732-0006
www.WesternLegendsResearch.com

Front cover image and book design by Dr. Dale Tunnell, Western Legends Research

Printed by Western Legends Research, in the United States of America

ISBN: 978-1-7334212-8-7

FIRST EDITION

Contents

Reader Bonus Offer

Are you curious about what occurs behind the scenes? I've constructed a website with additional information and videos that might help you. As a bonus for reading this book, I want to offer you some tips and shortcuts that may help you protect yourself against bad operators and political cronies. I continue to add new material, so I often return to review the latest and greatest.

I also put together a combination of eBooks, videos, and tools of interest. Head to my website and get free access to these little gems.

https://www.westernlegendsresearch.com/resources

Also, By Dale Tunnell, Ph.D.

1. Resurrecting the Dead
2. Decoding Treachery
3. Codename: Language Inquisitor
4. 1000 Confessions: Layered Voice Analysis for Investigators
5. Computerized Psychiatric Content Analysis and Diagnosis in an Investigative Environment in Computerized Content Analysis of Speech and Verbal Texts and its Many Applications

6. Voice Frequency Analysis of Cognitive Stress Differences Between Men and Women During an Episodic Deception Task

Dedication

I dedicate this book to my wife, Deborah, who has always supported, nurtured, and guided me in pursuing the truth.

Acknowledgments

I always include a list of individuals who have supported and mentored me in my books. My approach is somewhat different in this book. In the past, I listed those who helped me begin my journey in the field of Layered Voice Analysis.

Now, I want to thank those newly elected leaders who have jumped into the fire of politics. You appear at a time when our society needs fresh ideas and integrity. Your journey won't be easy; sometimes, it will be more disheartening than uplifting.

But if you can avoid corruption and political doubletalk, your involvement in the political process will benefit our country's constitutional fabric. Thank you for having the courage to take on this challenge.

Who Should Read This Book?

Like most books I write, I remove details that mask the book's intent so that you can read the book in one setting. I want you to gain insights as quickly and efficiently as possible. I don't want to waste your time if this book isn't a good fit for you.

Please read this entire section to see if *Politics and Betrayal: Layered Voice Analysis for Newly Elected Leaders* is a wise investment of your time to read further.

This book isn't for everyone, but I stand by the well-established concepts and practices supported by years of research and psychological studies.

My focus is on helping newly elected leaders gain powerful analytical resources so they can avoid political fraud and, at the same time, protect their reputations and credibility.

I think my suggestions should help you increase your protective capabilities. In my book, *Politics and Betrayal: Layered Voice Analysis for Newly Elected Leaders,* you will discover means to prevent political turmoil, corrupt affiliations that damage your credibility, and hidden malintent that can compromise your values.

Specifically, I created this book for two types of people:

- The citizen leader. You want to excel in representing the values and needs of your constituency and develop a proven track record of credibility and a valued reputation.

- The intuitive leader. You want your office to be successful and recognized for its superior credibility and unquestioned legislative abilities.

If you measure your success by accomplishment and skill, determination to excel, and a drive to successfully represent your constituency through legitimate legislative action, I wrote *Politics and Betrayal: Layered Voice Analysis for Newly Elected Leaders* for you.

I've met many politicians who don't have even a rudimentary understanding of human nature except to pad their bank accounts. They learned to speak without saying anything and answer questions without meaning by spinning their language. But they provide subconscious disclosures through their voices without knowing. And, with LVA, you can capture these details they don't want you to know.

However, please save time reading more if you are a politician in business for status and personal benefit. I didn't write this book for charlatans. This book is not for you.

No, I wrote this book for three reasons:

1. I want to shift your focus from simply being a mediocre political hack to becoming a prepared and leading specialist with critical skills superior to your contemporaries.

2. I want to provide insights not generally taught to laypersons that will help you predictably gain deep insight into opponents

and supporters of all types
and position you to become
a sought-after powerhouse of
leadership; and,

3. I want to let you know
about significant expertise that
will continue to benefit you
throughout your political career
as you develop your skills into an
art form.

Search for those resources that help you reach ethical conclusions on your own.

This book will provide a clear path to apply independent and legitimate reasoning and find solutions to the most demanding circumstances.

If you agree with these tenants, we are like-minded:

1. Establishing a good reputation, influence, and credibility takes work.

2. Learning fundamentals in any endeavor is the foundation from which to build expertise.

3. Becoming a professional in your newly elected position should be an eventual goal of any person who wishes for superior skills to solve problems for others.

If you desire to move out of your comfort zone, attain more skill, enhance your credibility, and reach a pinnacle of expertise you never thought possible, then I wrote *Politics and Betrayal: Layered Voice Analysis for Newly Elected Leaders* for you. **It would be best if you kept reading.**

My Promise to You

The importance of becoming a successfully elected leader in a function that is so diverse and yet incorporates so few experts is an endeavor worthy of anyone's goals.

If I can motivate you and open your intuitive mind, you will develop a sense of awareness as a "superior" leader. Confidence in your ability to recognize the power of patterns in speech and linguistic dynamics will strengthen your innate defenses and protect you from political corruption and bad actors.

An elected leader who correctly uses superior methodology with mindful dexterity generates decisiveness and consistency. When called upon, your talent will out-maneuver diatribe and political spin.

Implementing the processes outlined in this book will enhance your credibility and reputation as a recognized authority in negotiations and representation. At the same time, you gain superior insight into your opponents' cognitive functions and motivations. You will also attain a higher level of experience to minimize harmful exposure while you reach levels of expertise you may not have thought possible.

That is my promise to you!

Introduction

In all my years as a criminal investigator, educator, and LVA Operator, I've learned that, while occasionally predictable, human nature can shock you beyond belief. Sometimes, it's like shooting in the dark at a moving target. It can be an uncertain endeavor. Layered Voice Analysis (LVA) removes much of the uncertainty about the intent of others and the actions they take to protect themselves. A problem I discovered long ago is that if you are looking for a simple "yes" or "no" to determine truth or deception, you will miss lots of detail that will skew your decision-making and personal judgments.

Using LVA solely as a "lie detector" can be compared to killing ants with a sledgehammer. That narrow application of the LVA is counter-productive and under-utilizes its capacity. I equate LVA technology to a surgical tool. I apply the derivative applications to isolate details that will give me a holistic view of a person's motives, fears, emotions, feelings, what they hide, and why they obfuscate. The human mind is complex, with a database superior to any computer. LVA allows me to tap into this database and analyze the cognitive processes of the conscious mind in macro-detail. And it will do the same for you.

I now use LVA in the same manner that will help high-quality elected leaders protect themselves against the onslaught of political corruption. I am the only LVA master practitioner worldwide recognized for that distinction, and I am here to help you.

I encourage you to continue reading to learn how to create a layer of defense against dishonesty and corruption and evade falling into deceitful traps.

How Vulnerable Are You to Bribery?

Corruption is often motivated by a desire to obtain an unfair competitive advantage over others. Individuals or groups sometimes engage in bribery because they believe they deserve special treatment. In other instances, bribery occurs to level the playing field. For example, a corrupt government may pay bribes to foreign companies to ensure stable contracts.

In addition to bribery, several other reasons individuals or organizations engage in corruption exist. Some bribe recipients have no choice but to accept money for favors. Others may believe that accepting bribes is morally acceptable.

Finally, some people view corruption as a necessary evil. They see it as a way to meet ends in challenging times.

Factors That Facilitate Corruption

There are many people involved in legislated projects, including engineers and architects, surveyors, quantities surveyors, lawyers, accountants, auditors, bankers and finance directors, managers, supervisory personnel, supervisors, site officials, builders, electricians and plumbers, carpenters, bricklayers, plasters, tilers, roofing workers, decorators, glazing workers, joiners, plating workers, machining workers, drivers, laborers, and cleaners. The list of participants could go on forever. Corruption is frequently accepted and viewed as a way of life in the business world. As a result, corruption is widespread.

The World Bank says that many factors at the national level contribute to the deterioration of infrastructure projects. These include weak governance systems, poor transparency, ineffective enforcement mechanisms, inadequate laws and regulations, and insufficient financial resources.

The lack of consistent anticorruption policy in government undermines efforts to curb corruption. Public officials cannot know whether they act legally or illegally without clear rules and guidelines. In addition, more consistency in anticorruption policies necessitates clarity among stakeholders.

With clarity, it is easier to identify and report corruption cases.

For example, a lack of clarity around how much money should go into different budgets leads to the misappropriation of funds. Similarly, a lack of clarity around the roles and responsibilities of various departments and agencies makes it hard for authorities to ensure accountability.

The Electoral Consequences of Corruption

Political corruption is the misuse of government power for illegitimate private gain, including bribery, lobbying, extortion, and cronyism. But there are many different definitions of political corruption. Some people think it involves the abuse of public office for personal gain; others say it is about using influence over government policy for private profit. Still, others define it as the illegal exchange of money for favors. And some people simply call it corruption.

We tend to view political corruption in the United States as a problem primarily affecting developing countries, where powerful politicians exploit their positions for financial gain. Most research suggests that corruption harms economic growth. However, political corruption is a global phenomenon affecting both rich and emerging countries. It is often associated with authoritarian regimes, but even democratic governments can succumb to corruption. The current American citizenry is waking up to the concept that our country has become as corrupt as any other, especially in our election processes.

Although political corruption is widespread, the electoral consequences of crime are less clear. While some studies show that voters punish corrupt politicians, others find no effect. Moreover, scholars disagree about whether corruption hurts incumbents or challengers.

The reality is that once engaged, disengagement is nearly impossible. Bribery and corruption can take many forms. Sometimes doing a policy-breaking favor for someone is enough to jeopardize you. You never really know if the benefactor has your interest in mind, and quite often, they don't!

I saw this scenario play out in correctional facilities. An inmate asked an officer to do them a favor by violating some rule. Once the officer granted the request, the agreement escalated to more dramatic turns, which carried stiffer penalties for the employee. Eventually, the employee was fully compromised, facing suspension, expulsion, or even incarceration. Gender had no impact. Male and female officers were equally compromised, nearly always involving sympathy or graft.

It isn't just inmates who use sympathy against their victims. Unscrupulous politicians are famous for leveraging constituents' feelings for some underhanded concept or plan. As a newly elected leader, you must always be alert to deception and malintent. It may cause embarrassment if later discovered, but disclosure of a corrupt involvement (whether intended or not) can result in judicial sanctions, such as fines or incarceration.

While you must rely on your intuition, remember that it is not infallible. The stakes are high, and corruption needs only a minor slippage. It would be best if you had other mechanisms to protect you from those who would harm you and your credibility. I'll talk more on that subject in subsequent chapters.

What is Layered Voice Analysis (LVA)?

You evaluate what someone says and how they say it every time you communicate. Signals include volume, tone, clarity, and other factors. They indicate rage, fear, excitement, unpredictability, potential health issues, and drug or alcohol use. Most people regularly analyze other people's voices to determine their emotions and how they are expressed. LVA focuses on hints drawn from speech frequencies and time domains to assess emotions, mental state, and degree of honesty.

When speaking to others, we frequently choose a different voice to convey a particular emotion, such as happiness, firmness, uncertainty, or anger. Through our words and deeds, we constantly express our actual emotions. We strive to manage our voices so they won't reveal our genuine feelings, yet we often use them to communicate feelings that cover up real feelings hiding below them.

Traditionally, phonetic analysis has concentrated on the sounds people hear in speech. On the other hand, Layered Voice Analysis (LVA) listens more dynamically to the voice, picking up evidence of its uncontrolled aspects. One of these attributes is the genuine feelings people experience when expressing their opinions. Because thoughts are connected to voices by neural networks, it is possible to recognize thoughts and emotions by observing the deep voice parameters.

Nemesysco, the LVA developer, created new measurement methods to measure and quantify these sentiments. They serve as the foundation for the LVA's emotion detection technology. These algorithms work with baseline measurements in every emotion analysis assessment LVA measures!

Even though most of the LVAs' parameters are new, their expressed and enduring values occasionally may also have emotional analytic significance. We'll consider pertinent any vocal component with dynamic content for this conversation.

Layered Voice Analysis draws on various scientific disciplines to do multilayer voice analysis, including phonetics, psychology, psychophysiology, and neuroscience.

Become acquainted with the following terms related to the LVA:

Sensations are natural emotions we experience without the need for thought or reasoning. The three main tendencies of stress, exhilaration, and perplexity are included in the LVA technology. LVA technology in other forms also accounts for emotional energy as the fourth feeling.

Emotions are deeper representations of emotional reactions, frequently employed to describe how something is seen. They include nervousness, focus, anticipation, arousal, cognitive elevation, solemn contemplation, embarrassment, and imagination.

The traditional emotions—happy, sad, and angry—are considered "**expressions.**"

Your body's reaction to a threat is what we mean by **stress**. Your brain's amygdala detects a potential threat and alerts your body to get ready to take action. Then, your body goes into "survival mode" under the supervision of your ancient brain. Your immediate desire is to move away from the danger.

Stress is the reverse of excitement. You have a cheerful, energized feeling when you're enthusiastic. You might even experience anxiety as a result of your impatience.

The conflict between two or more opposing thoughts or beliefs is called cognitive stress or cognitive dissonance.

Inspirational ideas from psychologists during the 20th century may be somewhat recognizable. However, when categorizing emotions using LVA, these hypotheses are less pertinent.

Different classes were purposefully omitted by Nemesysco when developing the LVA. They didn't want to get bogged down in neatly categorizing things; instead, they tried to stick to the information gathered through daily activities.

Gathering accurate field data was a critical and essential step in understanding LVA, its special powers, and its limitations.

At this point, I'd like to explain a necessary concern for you to consider. By its very nature, voice analysis is a sensitive process. The LVA is easily influenced by background noise and input volume. LVA indications are influenced by the quality of the equipment, the compression methods, and the environmental stimuli the test subjects are exposed.

These variables can considerably impact how much information we glean from the audio recording. Despite these drawbacks, LVA can still extract helpful information from almost all audio signals. However, each phase of the analysis process must be carried out with caution and common sense.

What is the Deceptive Circuit?

The majority of the time, when we have a sensation, it is either pleasant (excitement), negative (stress), or we are unsure of it (Confusion, Cognitive Stress). A feeling will typically only move in one direction. The only exception is lying.

When a decision is made, deceptive circuits begin to form a divergence from the sensation's natural course. When someone anticipates an unfavorable outcome, they try to alter it by lying or withholding information. This realization is a significant development and represents "changing one's future (outcome)." The process is simultaneously exhilarating, perplexing, and problematic. Feelings become volatile and visible to LVA.

LVA is a very advanced technology that uses algorithmic analysis to measure psychological states and then statistically displays the results. I mentioned that the LVA measures about 150 aspects of the human voice. That figure is conservative. It provides a functional operating level for the time being. Practitioners add more dimensions and definitions as research expands, revealing previously unknown intricacies and dynamics that are superior to those we already know.

Currently, a sizeable number of operators worldwide use an LVA variant application in some way. The cost of the system ranges from a few thousand dollars for commercial software to well over $50,000 for the more sophisticated security and investigation capabilities. When you ask an LVA operator for help, they frequently provide information you wouldn't find on your own.

But remember that despite their training, these operators are not master practitioners, of which there are only three worldwide. You now have a book prepared by the only Master Practitioner of Layered Voice Analysis who deploys it for personal defense. I reside in the United States and am available for frank dialogue anytime. I might make recommendations you wouldn't have thought about, but my time is never wasted by helping you.

How Does Layered Voice Analysis Work?

Every facet of our lives—from job decisions to intimate relationships to scientific discoveries, from infancy to maturity, childhood to adulthood, and adolescence to old age—has been hampered by the difficulty of comprehending human emotions and motivations. We can react and engage with others more skillfully as we understand human emotions and motivations. The novel technology distributed by Nemesysco was created in 1997 by Amir Lieberman.

Nemesysco regularly works with specialists from various pertinent sectors as part of its ongoing development. These include linguistics, mathematics, phonetics, medicine, psychiatry, psychology, and criminal justice. The LVA focuses on detecting fraudulent intentions in real-world scenarios and the unpredictable yet phonetic features of the human voice.

The system works by correlating a patented set of vocal metrics with particular human emotions and detecting dishonest intent simultaneously. These voice factors were discovered by listening to audio files recorded in various environments and languages, including call centers, controlled tests, and police interrogations. Numerous LVA technology parameters are new in phonetics, focusing on the erratic but speech-related characteristics of the human voice.

Layered Voice Analysis, the foundational technology of Nemesysco, has been adapted for use in numerous professional settings, including police investigations, fraud control, security clearance screening, hiring, personality testing, quality control monitoring, intelligence gathering, lawful interception, and so forth.

"Lie Detection" and LVA

A lie is still a lie, whether it is discovered or not. Lie detection incorporates several physiological falsehoods, each calling for an unusual but detectable reaction. A single feature cannot distinguish fiction from the truth. We can only define a lie as a statement made intentionally false, while truthfulness is stating something without understanding it may be wrong.

No one is perfect, of course. Everybody occasionally lies, especially when we are anxious. We typically catch ourselves lying and work to fix the problem. Although figuring out whether a particular statement is true or false is tricky. It's one of the reasons why the LVA prioritizes emotional patterns over lie detection. To distinguish between cognitive effort and distortion, we study patterns. We already understand the meaning behind the distinctive qualities of the designs, but the LVA is necessary to make them apparent.

The "Emotional Diamond."

To clarify and display the complicated human emotional reaction complexity discovered by Layered Voice Analysis, Nemesysco developed the Emotional

Diamond idea in 2012. The concept originated from finding out that people's emotional reactions change based on their circumstances. Determining someone's true thoughts or feelings might be challenging unless you ask them directly. And when they answer, actual thoughts and feelings may be intentionally masked.

Many companies utilize questionnaires to determine how their staff feel about a particular subject. However, these methods usually entail lengthy interviews that demand little time and effort. So how does one find information about someone else without explicitly asking them?

Examining voice replies to open-ended inquiries is the key to finding the solution. It is a form of speech-based communication that enables people to express themselves naturally. LVA is not language-dependent. Instead, regardless of the language being spoken, LVA can evaluate any verbal conversation. As a result, the ability to recognize emotional states is broad. Nemesysco developed the Emotional Diamond as part of the LVA process to help those who want to comprehend the dynamic mental processes of others. This tool is based on the premise that every emotion has a unique shape. Examining the diamond's shape may determine if a positive or negative sentiment is being expressed. The diamond can also offer details about the strength of each emotion.

Is There Proof That Layered Voice Analysis Actually Works?

There have been several studies around the globe that evaluated the validity and reliability of Layered Voice Analysis. I suggest you visit Nemesysco's website at https://www.nemesysco.com/technology/research.... You can look over several quality studies from around the globe on the efficacy of Layered Voice Analysis. There are many comprehensive studies, and you will agree when you read them that LVA is an impressive software technology.

On a more personal note, I conducted a study in a correctional facility involving 900 inmates and 15000 phone calls over six months. The results were impressive and led to contraband seizures, identification of assaultive personnel, and criminal activity beyond the institution's walls. The data belonged to the institution, and no formal presentation occurred even though the results were substantial. Still, the study proved to me there were substantiated benefits to using Layered Voice Analysis.

More in line with the political environment and the need for protection from those who could harm your credibility and reputation, I performed numerous analyses of political figures of late using the LVA 6.50. Three, in particular, came to mind immediately. I analyzed one speech by President Joe Biden when he defended *The Inflation Reduction Act* on July 28, 2022. In the second speech, Speaker of the House Nancy Pelosi presented remarks after returning from her trip to Taiwan. And to be fair, I also analyzed comments provided by House Minority Leader Kevin McCarthy regarding plans for the GOP after Midterm Elections in the United States.

Before I give you the LVA birds-eye view of those speeches and comments, I want to address something you may be curious about. I've heard comments that many political speeches are written by someone else for the politician. So how is it possible to analyze a politician's speech written by someone else?

The answer is complex, but I'll try to simplify it. The human mind comprises many functions, but the conscious and subconscious levels are two of the most relevant. The conscious level controls "here and now" activity. The subconscious level controls your senses and all autonomic activity, i.e., heart rate, respiration, nervous system, etc.

If someone writes a speech for you, you must read it using a teleprompter or other means. Your conscious level takes in the data; simultaneously, the subconscious analyzes it. This relationship is cognitive processing.

The data, having been processed, produces feelings and emotions about what you read. Regardless of the context of the speech, your mind has already analyzed it in nanoseconds. The cognitive process chooses to trust or distrust the speech content. When you speak, your neural network communicates the cognitive processing through the voice for analysis by LVA. Since LVA is not language-dependent, the words and story are irrelevant. Only the voice matters.

In other words, the written slant of the speech or story is unremarkable. All that matters to the LVA is what your cognitive assessment produces and communicates via your voice.

President Joe Biden

President Biden's Inflation Reduction Act speech consisted of 4,164 analyzed segments. Three thousand eight hundred seventy-two (3,862) elements were flagged as problems relating to inaccuracies and falsehoods. His profile suggests a significant cognitive impairment, but that isn't new. In my book, "Codename: Language Inquisitor," I addressed President Biden's mental capacity in more detail.

He presented with an abnormally high imagination, which may account for many of the concocted stories about his youth. Mental and emotional states were unstable, along with high stress and feelings of guilt. This detail adequately coincides with what we have already learned about President Biden.

Speaker of the House Nancy Pelosi

Nancy Pelosi journeyed to Taiwan when political relationships between the United States, China, and Taiwan were particularly fragile. The motives for her trip were unclear, and her timing seemed rushed. The Chinese government reacted negatively to her journey and conducted a show-of-force military exercise against Taiwan, amassing troops, ships, aircraft, and missiles. An LVA 6.50 analysis suggested she was exhausted from her travels and somewhat disjointed in her presentation, with unstable cognition and emotional states. Out of sixty-three analyzed segments, nine were calculated as high-risk-false comments. Three comments stood out among the others and might be relevant for further investigation.

First, a segment containing "...peace in the Taiwan Strait" indicated she believes peace may not exist. Second, "...our friendship with Taiwan is a strong one" suggests a high-risk falsehood. My subjective review highlights her disbelief in this statement, as well. Third, "...they are not doing our travel schedule...the Chinese Government," indicated concealment. All three comments recorded a deception category of "Embarrassment Lies." As demonstrated, LVA 6.50 isolated three very interesting phrases for further investigation.

Considering that military exercises take months to prepare, it becomes relevant to ask whether or not Nancy Pelosi's journey to Taiwan was used as an excuse to conduct such activities and whether she the Chinese coerced her to take the trip. However, the high-risk samples identified above should be scrutinized further. Is there a reason for embarrassment? Nancy Pelosi's husband, Paul, has significant financial interests in China. Could that relationship have some bearing on her trip? Is our relationship with Taiwan that strong? I can think of numerous questions relevant to her journey.

Inquiry is what LVA creates. It is an investigation-focus tool that highlights areas of interest and further investigation. In this instance, the LVA didn't so much answer these questions; it brought focus to questions that should have been asked.

Kevin McCarthy

Kevin McCarthy's remarks about what he considered necessary for the Republican Party to accomplish after the midterm election consisted of eight hundred eighty-six segments. LVA 6.50 analysis flagged two hundred thirty-seven mid- to high-risk segments. None were flagged as "false." However, all flagged segments fell into an "Embarrassment Lie" category.

Because of the number of high-risk assignments with none classified as false, I turned to content analysis of his comments to determine the cause. In each flagged instance, McCarthy referred to failures by President Biden and his administration to protect the American people regarding COVID-19, inflation, the southwest border, energy production, and the deadly impact of fentanyl trafficked by the cartels. His position on each of these issues was one of embarrassment. Whether McCarthy's assessments were accurate or not, his emotional and cognitive views of these issues resulted in instability in cognition, emotions, anxiety, and intensified stress.

There is one other issue that rose above the others. Much of the stress he is feeling is about ascending to the role of Speaker of the House. There may be some self-doubt about whether or not he can do the job. But more than that, he may focus more on getting the job than serving his constituency. Of course, one has to get the job before he can do the job.

I conducted analyses of numerous other public figures using the same methods I would use to help you. Layered Voice Analysis provides a wealth of linguistic, emotional, and psychological detail, like accessing an open library. No matter the topic, LVA lifts the cloak of concealment and shines a light on hidden emotions and cognitive processes. Despite attempts at deception, the voice is a pathway to subconscious self-betrayal, and LVA recognizes it.

When Should You Deploy Layered Voice Analysis Applications?

Without equivocation, I believe the best time to deploy either the LVA technology or the skill of a Master Practitioner is when you first question the motive or actions of someone with whom you have interacted. Don't doubt your intuition because something has stirred your instincts. It would be best if you acted on intuition. People tend to ignore their internal warning signs because they believe they're being silly. Or they fail to comprehend the meanings of threats and intimidation. Often they confuse a collegial and charming personality with hidden malintent and concealment of true intentions. People who succumb to con artists can't get beyond that smile and smooth demeanor even though their instincts tell them to be careful.

Don't get me wrong. Instincts and intuition fail occasionally but generally err on the side of protection. Layered Voice Analysis is a check and balance technology. Whether you were right and discovered an exchange was fraught with danger or you were wrong and the interaction was cordial and legitimate, LVA provides you with insight to recognize the difference.

There is one issue I have to address. LVA requires the medium of the human voice to conduct an analysis. How do you analyze someone who is speaking to you? Unless you deploy LVA as a security tool or human resources application, you probably can't pull out your computer and ask the person you are talking with to submit to a computer-driven question-and-answer session. You'll need a recording of the person's voice so you can complete the analysis offline at a later date or time. There are a couple of ways to obtain a recording:

- Retrieve records from public venues where the person has addressed the same issues. Radio spots, television interviews, and recorded segments uploaded to Youtube or other social media platforms are excellent sources.

- Record the conversation yourself with a digital recorder. Surreptitious recording may be illegal in your state, so don't secretly record the conversation. Be upfront and ask if the person would mind you recording your conversation. Having a policy to document all business dialog is a good idea. Instead of saying the recording is for training purposes like call centers do, you could tell your visitor(s) you use the recording to review comments to make sure you have covered all bases and to review proposals. If they refuse your request, it is a good bet there will be something in the conversation they don't want to go public. This is a clue to which you should pay attention. In the event of a refusal, you can continue the conversation, but please keep in mind there is a sensitive issue on the table.

- You may also wish to record telephone conversations, but the

> same rules apply to you. Could you notify the person that you are recording the exchange for later review? Again, if you have a recording policy in place, people get used to it. At the same time, you have established yourself as someone serious about your public responsibilities and protective of your integrity.

Once you have a digital recording, you can deploy an LVA application you purchased or send it to an LVA operator for analysis. Either way, you will be able to have your answer as to the trustworthiness of your visitor in a short time.

How Do I Decide Which LVA Methods to use?

I wrote a book titled *1000 Confessions: Layered Voice Analysis for Investigators* at a time when investigators worldwide were trying to cut through a deluge of information and sort between what was accurate and what was inaccurate. I described several programs that were derivatives of the LVA technology. These included **InTone**, **InTone with RA7 A.I.**, **LVA-i**, and the **LVA 6.50**. The first three programs were designed for commercial operations, including call centers, insurance companies, customer service, and human resources. **LVA 6.50** is an aggressive investigations focus tool for law enforcement and security investigations. The Israel Ministry of Defense tightly controls the dissemination of the program, and it is expensive. Also, this application is seldom sold to individuals because of government controls.

If you were to attempt a do-it-yourself and purchase LVA software, I recommend the **LVA-i**. It has the least expensive, stand-alone desktop capability and requires minimal training. But without training and a complete understanding of the overall technology, your results might be ineffective, or you may misinterpret those results. You can also reach out to me, and I will help you find the best solution for you. You are probably busy enough that taking on an operator's role might be burdensome. Expense and time are considerations. It all depends on how often you need to deploy the application.

If you want to avoid a steep learning curve and need a comprehensive evaluation with a short turnaround, I recommend finding an LVA operator to help you. There are some in North America, and a call to Nemesysco might help you gain access to these operators. But they are neither Master Practitioners nor Level III authorized trainers. I carry both distinctions and am the best person to help you.

What Methods of Inquiry Do You Employ?

In all my years as an investigator, I learned that, like people, machines make mistakes regardless of the sophistication and level of programming. If humans are involved, no program or device is infallible. Consequently, I allow myself all the advantages I can procure to limit interpretive errors and biases. My primary platform is the LVA 6.50. Even though Nemesysco will eventually phase out the program and replace it with something more inclusive, I intend to use that program until they do so.

The intricacies of the LVA 6.50 are sometimes difficult to comprehend, but the output of in-depth data far exceeds that produced by the other programs. This is by design, however. The engine of all LVA products is what they refer to as LVA7. Nemesysco controls output based on the commercial needs and combinations of services for any particular business. Since LVA 6.50 is an investigative tool dealing with severe criminal and security issues, it must be robust and operate with specificity. The detail obtained from the LVA 6.50 is unnecessary in most commercial applications.

So, as I stated, LVA 6.50 is my investigation tool of choice. I also use three other tools for verification and validation. This is a personal choice, and while LVA 6.50 produces comprehensive data, it never hurts to have other means of review. "Trust but Verify!" When I was in the Army a half-century ago, I worked for an agency with the motto, "In God We Trust; All Others We Monitor." I think that motto applies nicely to LVA.

A strong background in psychology provides my foundation. Additionally, the three programs I employ consist of the following:

- Psycholinguistic Patterning
- Content Analysis
- Psychiatric Content Analysis and Diagnosis.

I will describe all three applications in the following chapters. At this point, I need to say that none of the three were easy to master, and I don't expect any layperson to attempt to do so. I'm not talking about learning these three applications in weeks or months but in years. Chances are, you won't need this level of review, so attempting to master these applications is probably overkill. But when you need help, the intensity of the problem may dictate how you approach it. Procuring the service of a Master Practitioner may be preferable to going it alone. I always found that working as a team was more effective than working alone. You experience fewer mistakes, and you learn as you go.

What Is Psycholinguistic Patterning?

2018 saw the publication of a brief explanation of this method on my website, www.westernlegendsresearch.com. I've added it below as a cure for insomnia!

It is necessary to use specific analytical techniques to investigate the accuracy of the data and the impact of any psychological variables that might affect validity. The integrity of verbal information can be verified today using various widely accepted and popular procedures.

These techniques serve as examples of some linguistic, lexical, and word usage observations. Since the early 1960s, fundamental linguistic principles have been used to assess verbal and written interaction in social sciences and humanities disciplines while frequently examined subjectively.

Linguistic techniques share common standards. Purposeful or unintentional thinking sparked by memory stimuli results in physiological and vocal responses, both of which can be recognized through physical observation or language analysis.

Language analyses offer an excellent range of information contexts for evaluation. Linguistic techniques advise that the participants' lexical definitions and word counts be determined linguistically; they should also serve as a foundation for a much more thorough assessment, including the psychiatric diagnosis reflecting behavioral responses.

Examining psychological behavior should offer more than just a picture of how verbal communication turned out in a much larger environment. I know this is really dry information, and I probably lost you. Still, linguistic techniques should detect pathology, anxiety, depression, aggression, health-sickness problems, and other mental consequences in addition to the word meanings in the statement's content.

Is There a Psychiatric Disorder?

To prove the presence of psychiatric disease, it is essential to understand that when we investigate statements, we are not looking for a clinical diagnosis. The analyst is not typically a clinical practitioner. So, we are not trying to treat an individual. A specialist might be able to recognize a psychological trend with the comment, though.

This approach enables the examiner to formulate a statement's validity using more data. In other words, when the communication was made, was the person in control of their faculties, or did they have a psychological or cognitive impairment?

With a tool to aid in the reasoned analysis, mental problems could be evident to an analyst. However, the usefulness of the information presented may significantly change if a mental disorder is present. Remember that a person's psychological state does not immediately rule out the validity of the information they supply.

What is Content Analysis?

Analysis of Textual Information

Content Analysis examines text-based materials like books, articles, web pages, movies, etc. This procedure entails classifying and summarizing the text after reading and understanding it. As you may expect, the type of document being examined determines the best method for text analysis.

I apply the LVA to a voice recording and then perform relational analysis. The LVA frequently picks up verbal cues about the person speaking or discussing the topic. Unintentional subconscious disclosures (USD) or other relationships to time and space could be the source of the verbal clues. Additionally, I transcribe talks to visually examine the meanings of words and phrases and how they relate.

I also do semantic analysis, seeking out associations between ideas and words. A concept is a sign that conveys information by connecting to other characters. We investigate how one thing relates to another in relational studies. According to a relational analysis, relationships, objects, and processes are the three essential parts of cognition. Links join things together, while objects are what you think about, and functions are how you feel. A relational analysis displays the relationships between these components using graphs or networks. You can better comprehend how individuals think after reading this analysis.

Experts employ relational analyses in various disciplines, including psychology, linguistics, education, sociology, anthropology, history, marketing, and advertising. Relational studies can examine communication, including emails, social media posts, online articles, books, and text messages.

Relational Analysis involves looking for text patterns. Finding connections between various pieces of information, including words, phrases, sentences, paragraphs, etc., and coding those linkages into something meaningful are both parts of this process. You might be interested in learning which word combinations are most common or which subjects are covered by particular authors. You may even try to define why specific phrases are used.

I bring up the significance of patterns once more. A relational analysis's objective is to find patterns in the data. These patterns could reveal information about linguistic usage, document structure, or human behavior. They can aid in responding to inquiries like: What can I learn about my audience from this document? How effectively do I interact with this group? Why did this remark get posted?

Issues of Reliability & Validity

Content analysis also examines what individuals say regarding various subjects in text and video media. Instead of numbers or data points, this type of research, known as qualitative research, concentrates on the meaning of words, phrases, and sentences. Researchers employ content analysis to understand better how people express their thoughts and emotions. They examine the structure and organization of messages. We can recognize patterns and trends in communication thanks to content analysis. For instance, we can ask what the author means when they employ specific terminology. How do authors structure their paragraphs of information? What causes the writing's tone to evolve? We could even investigate if men and women write about various topics differently.

Studies utilizing content analysis come in a variety of forms. Concept mapping is one of the most common methods for researchers to create a study topic model. Discourse analysis is another strategy that looks at language structure. Another is a rhetorical analysis, which examines how arguments are structured. Last but not least, textual analysis investigates the written word itself.

Advantages of Content Analysis

Content analysis is a frequently used concept that needs to be fully understood. But it's not that difficult. It's merely text analysis done well. The textual analysis seeks to identify patterns in data. For instance, you might be curious to discover whether specific terms frequently occur together. Or perhaps you're curious about how often different phrases are related to one another. Natural Language Processing is used for textual analysis (NLP) and offers extensive unstructured text analysis.

How do I use Content Analysis?

I apply content analysis similarly to other analysts. I examine materials that have been transcribed and look for trends. However, I usually already know what these patterns signify since I use established standards that I have been accustomed to over several years. By following predetermined criteria, my assessment—while occasionally time-consuming—achieves a more thorough grasp of the emotional dynamics at work. In my book, “Decoding Treachery,” which is available on Amazon.com, I distilled these standards. The information is a crucial resource for anyone looking for an easy way to distinguish fact from fiction.

Psychiatric Content Analysis and Diagnosis (PCAD3) is a computer program that I also use to validate any psychological discoveries that the LVA results might reveal. For instance, if the LVA identifies cognitive deterioration, I might use PCAD3 to check if the same outcomes appear. I combined these two ideas when I examined Vice President Joe Biden in 2018. Both applications showed signs of cognitive deterioration, but many of his supporters tried to conceal what was ultimately extremely clear, even to those without background knowledge. Does it matter if, for public reasons, we distinguish between dementia and senility? There is cognitive deterioration either way.

What is Psychiatric Content Analysis and Diagnosis?

Psychiatric Content Analysis and Diagnosis (PCAD-3) has been used successfully with neuropsychiatric assessments. Scales that measure different emotional and psychobiological states are valid and reliable in much real-world research. There are external anger and anxiety scales (which have subscales for death, mutilation, separation, guilt, and diffuse fear). The Anxiety Scale identifies six types of anxiety: general anxiety, fear of death, fear of being cut, fear of being alone, fear of being responsible, and fear of shame. Both mutilation anxiety and castration anxiety are the same things though I have only seen this in one analysis.

The three kinds of hate that the Hostility Scales measure don't have long-term effects. The Cognitive and Intellectual Impairment Scale measures changes in a person's cognitive and intellectual functioning and finds long-lasting and irreversible deficits. The Hope Scale measures a person's certainty that things will turn out well. The Human Relations Scale measures a person's ability and desire to have good relationships with other people.

Since there are no standards and research is still ongoing, the Narcissistic Scale should be seen as an experiment.

The fact that doctors and therapists use speech a lot as a data source led to the creation of a system that can estimate the scope of different psychological dimensions from natural language in an objective and reliable way. The content analysis method for measuring psychological aspects takes the best parts of the self-report and observer rating scale approaches and puts them together.

The PCAD-3 method for analyzing content went through a careful process of development. Language theory, psychoanalytic clinic theory, and behavioral and conditioning theory are the theoretical bases for this assessment strategy. The PCAD-3 is used in neuropsychiatry and psychology to measure several things. People with medical conditions like diabetes or breast cancer are given these tests to determine how they feel emotionally.

The assessment is often completed when the patient needs to be more forthcoming.

To What Extent Do You Advise Using These Instruments?

Analytical outcomes can be astounding when you use LVA and add secondary evaluations like Content Analysis and PCAD3. Other than some highly-classified operations handled by the National Security Administration or another intelligence organization, I don't believe anything else is comparable. Speaking from my experience and lacking access to other systems of a similar nature, the sophistication of emotive investigation is unmatched.

I've been using the LVA and related programs for over fifteen years. I have discovered no technique better than the LVA and its offshoot programs. Asking for help from someone who is an expert in the intricacies and investigative capabilities of the LVA is something you should consider if you need business intelligence, investigation support, or a way to protect yourself from corruption and political manipulation.

I regularly receive requests for examples of how I use the LVA. I successfully solved cases using this approach as a criminal investigator. In a correctional setting, I also studied an LVA derivative program once referred to as the SCA1 and discovered illegal acts and inappropriate administrative behavior that resulted in legal sanctions and administrative penalties. I now concentrate on the activities of prominent politicians, public figures, and media types. Some of these characters are discussed in my book "Codename: Language Inquisitor," which is available on Amazon.com.

I wrote the book as a satirical evaluation of individuals like Prince Andrew, the Duke of York (who is no longer a member of the royal family), Joe and Hunter Biden, Adam Schiff, Devin Nunes, Nancy Pelosi, Donald J. Trump, and others. I didn't disclose in total what their analyses indicated, but there was enough for readers to conclude. Although I lightheartedly presented the LVA's capabilities in the book, I did suggest the sinister potential of these characters without calling them, outright liars.

So, should I encourage newly elected leaders to participate in this program?

I'm in favor of doing so, but with a proviso. Stay away from cognitive and emotive investigations if you are not committed to discovering what your opponents and critics are hiding. People often keep certain information from you because they might not want to hurt you. Not everything should be subject to disclosure. Also, I don't think anyone without the necessary training should use the LVA. Your results will be far from exceptional, and you won't be satisfied.

On the other hand, if you need expedited help, please don't hesitate to contact me. It will only cost you a phone call. A free, honest talk about your issue and potential fixes may help ease your worries.

The Next Step

Congratulations! You have made progress In protecting both yourself and your new career. I hope I've helped you consider self-protection from a different angle and that you are willing to work with me.

Think about how it will make you feel to know that you have taken steps to protect your reputation, credibility, and beliefs. It might give you the confidence to know whether or not the individual you are dealing with can be trusted, cares about the general public, and has your best interests in mind.

I wrote this book, as I previously indicated, for three main reasons:

1. To change your focus from being just another politician to becoming a well-known and prominent specialist with superior critical skills.

2. To give you information that politicians don't typically possess. The data will enable you to thoroughly understand your supporters and detractors of all stripes and position yourself to become a powerful legislator.

3. To educate you on the essential knowledge that will help as you hone your abilities and turn into a true professional.

Could you please consider and answer these three questions?

- Would you feel more at ease if you

knew you could trust an associate?

- Do you believe your principles, reputation, and credibility are worth preserving?

- Do you value having a professional by your side to offer guidance, act as a buffer and help you guard against hurtful smears and critical information in your new position?

If your responses were yes, yes, and yes, you currently have three options.

1. You can put this book away and ignore my advice. (I hope you don't go with this one.)

2. You can use the knowledge I provided.

3. Avoid using poor judgment by being cautious about dishonest people. Set up

a strategy session with me to go over your particular circumstance.

By selecting the third option, you have nothing to lose if you are serious about safeguarding yourself. The power of prediction and confirmation exists inside this one call.

Your objectives are particular to you. The goal of the conversation is to help you figure out whether working together is a good fit for both of us. Let's collaborate. Possibly not. But we won't know until we have this crucial discussion.

So that you know, this is not a sales call. The call is a two-way interview to ensure that we both think this is a good match.

You can ask me questions, and I'll ask you some. From there, we proceed. Typically, this call lasts between 20 and 30 minutes, but we'll keep talking until you're sure you're ready to work with me or you're ready to hang up.

You are not obligated to do anything.

Your morals, ethics, reputation, and trustworthiness are essential to you. I feel the same way about my skills. These calls are the perfect litmus tests to determine if we are a good fit. It's an opportunity to meet and decide whether cooperating makes sense.

So that you know – the onus is on you to respond to this call to action. Please make an appointment with me right now. Please make an appointment if you enjoyed what you read and feel like working closely with me to protect against deceit and political corruption. There is absolutely no cost, commitment, risk, or obligation.

How to Set Up Our Phone Call

What you should do is:

1. Email me at dtunnell@westernlegendsresearch.com and express your interest or ask for a call.

2. We can set a time for either a chat on the phone or a zoom call.

I'm eager to hear from you and, more importantly, to work with you to keep you safe from dishonest politicians and bad political actors.

Thank you,

Dr. Dale Tunnell

PS. If you are interested in training or purchasing a particular LVA application, please contact Nemesysco, Ltd. These folks will be happy to help you
and answer any questions about their technology or applications.

Author's Bio

DR. DALE TUNNELL was born in Powell, Wyoming, in 1951. He is a decorated Vietnam veteran, married, and now living a retired lifestyle in Wright, Wyoming.

Trained in Layered Voice Analysis, Psycholinguistics, and Psychiatric Content Analysis and Diagnosis, Dale is a retired law enforcement officer with over forty years of service with federal, state, and local agencies. He earned his Master of Arts Degree in Management from Webster University and his Doctor of Philosophy Degree in Psychology from Capella University.

Dale received Beginning, Advanced, and Stage II training in Scientific Content Analysis (SCAN) from Avinoam Sapir at the Laboratory for Scientific Interrogation (LSI) in Phoenix, Arizona, and became an instructor for LSI.

Louis Gottschalk, MD, Ph.D., of the University of California at Irvine, from whom he acquired his expertise in measuring psychological states through content analysis of verbal behavior, mentored Dale while he worked on his doctorate. Dale later co-authored a book about computerized content analysis with Dr. Gottschalk and Dr. Robert Bechtel.

Dale became a research associate at the University of Arizona, *Center for Information, Technology, and Research (CITeR)*. Joining the Center's collaborative research efforts with federal agencies and American academic institutions, he advanced Layered

Voice Analysis studies and refined his practitioner skills.

After retiring from law enforcement, Halcyon Group International, a Department of Defense contractor, employed Dale as the Forensic Intelligence and Research Director.

He is the author of six books and an active member of the National Army Security Agency Association, the American Psychological Association, and the Linguistic Society of America.

Reader's Bonus Offer

Are you curious about what occurs behind the scenes? I've constructed a website with additional information and videos that might help you. As a bonus for reading this book, I want to offer you some tips and shortcuts that may help you protect yourself against bad operators and political cronies. I continue to add new material, so I often return to review the latest and greatest.

I also put together a combination of eBooks, videos, and tools of interest. Head to my website and get free access to these little gems.

www.westernlegendsresearch.com/reso
urces

A Small Request

I appreciate you taking the time to read *Politics and Betrayal: Layered Voice Analysis for Newly Elected Leaders*. If you take my advice, you will have a greater chance of avoiding the political traps and minefields associated with less-than-ideal political operators.

But would you do something for me? Please give this book an honest review on Amazon.com.

The BEST way for people to pick what books to buy is through reviews. I read through every review to find suggestions for improvement.

Email me at dtunnell@westernlegendsresearch.com if you have any questions or want to let me know what you think of *Politics and Betrayal: Layered Voice Analysis for Newly Elected Leaders*. I will appreciate hearing from you.